SUMMARY

Evicted

Matthew Desmond

Poverty and Profit

in the American City

Epic-Summary

Epic Summary LLC

© Copyright 2019 - Present.
All rights reserved.

Before we proceed...

Feel free to follow us on Facebook & Instagram for more summaries:

Instagram: https://www.instagram.com/bookingsuccess

TABLE OF CONTENTS

INTRODUCTION

Evicted: Poverty and Profit in the American City is a book written by Matthew Desmond. The book is about eviction and the side-effects that eviction can have on a person or community.

Eviction, which involves poverty and the loss of everything that a person once knew, has an enormous emotional impact on a person. When someone loses their home it is hard, if not impossible, to continue on living, because there are many things which inevitably follow and none of them are positive. That is why the author decided to write about these things that unfortunately become part of people's lives. The shelter, or home, is something that all of us want to have and something that we are ready to defend even with our lives. For this reason, when people lose their home, it creates a huge impact on them. Some of them recover and eventually find a job and a new life, but some people never recover and remain homeless.

There are two main characters in this book. One of them is a landlord named Sherrena Tarver, who rents houses for those who cannot afford to rent for themselves. The other one is a man named Tobin Charney, who runs a trailer park. The rest of the book is about sociological studies into the problem of eviction.

The book presents us with interesting insight into the lives of those who lost everything and its sociological dimension makes it very inviting literature.

SUMMARY

PART 1:
THERE ARE MORE EVICTIONS NOW THAN EVER BEFORE

The author opens the book by describing and comparing the situations regarding evictions during the time of the Depression and now. He states that during the Depression, evictions would bring masses of people who would form an organized resistance, but today is a lot different. Back then, many neighbors would prevent marshals from forcing families from their homes and taking their belongings, and law enforcement officers did not want to throw people out of their homes.

But now, in modern times, the situation has changed drastically. Evictions are something that happens almost every day. According to the author's calculations and research, in the late 2000s in Milwaukee there were approximately sixteen families evicted on a daily basis. In Georgia, 200,000 evictions were filed in 2017 alone, and in San Francisco, evictions increased by 38 percent between 2010 and 2013.

After this, the author writes about the personal consequences of eviction. Some of these are loss of possessions and loss of financial income. Children of evicted parents will either have to move to a different school or they miss school altogether. Many times when a person loses their home, they also lose their job. Eventually evictions may lead to depression, anxiety, drug and alcohol abuse, and similar problems. People are terrified by the event surrounding the eviction and because of that they are even more scared to face the future and what it holds. There are other situations where people have different health problems which can affect and be affected by evictions. Overall, evictions are part of a vicious circle: while evictions cause poverty, poverty is also the main cause for eviction.

In the next chapter of the book, the author discusses the Milwaukee area specifically, and the extreme discrimination present in evictions that take place there.

PART 2:
THE SEGREGATION
IN AMERICAN CITIES

This chapter opens with a description of the demonstrators who protested housing discrimination back in 1967. After their protest, Congress passed the Fair Housing Act, which outlawed discrimination housing. Despite this law, discrimination still exists in Milwaukee and housing remains largely segregated. That segregation means many things: one such example is that African-American families are often relegated to the North Side, while white families are concentrated on the South Side. And while many white renters are not so happy with the idea of renting a house in a neighborhood located in the area where many African-American people live, the same things happens with African-American renters, who are often not able to get housing in the area where white people live. In this way, landlords continue to discriminate against African-American tenants.

Unfortunately, segregation in housing is not limited to the Milwaukee area. There are still examples of segregation in Chicago, despite some recent improvements.

According to the author's research, in 2000, the average white person in Chicago lived in a neighborhood which was about 79 percent white. By 2016, that number had dropped to 71.5 percent. Also in 2000, the average African-American person lived in a neighborhood that was roughly 72 percent black, but at the present time this number had decreased to 64 percent.

The situation regarding segregation in Chicago is a bit different than in other cities and parts of the United States of America. African-American communities in Milwaukee,

Chicago and in cities like Philadelphia suffer serious consequences because of segregation. Some of these are being cut off from public transportation, being discriminated against in their workplaces, and suffering from discrimination regarding affordability of healthier food. Also, as the author states, the segregated population is easier to isolate and ignore. This means that this population will also be isolated and ignored when it comes to economic access, education and politics. And this is exactly the reason why segregation has long been a very powerful contributor to poverty.

PART 3:
EVICTIONS MAKE NEIGHBORHOODS UNSAFE AND DANGEROUS

This chapter is about how evictions make our neighborhoods unsafe and dangerous environments.

If we have poor neighborhoods which are strongly connected to each other, meaning that the people who live there have a strong sense of community, there will be a lot less crime than if there is little or no sense of community. But the bad thing is that evictions crumble and undermine this sense of community, whether the people are wealthy or poor. When people constantly fear for their lives and constantly worry about whether or not they will they get evicted from their homes, they do not "invest" themselves enough in their neighborhoods. The overall conclusion is that these neighborhoods will thus have more crime. With time, these neighborhoods will deteriorate even more, and the people who live there will sink further and further into poverty.

After this, the author mentions *The Death and Life of Great American Cities*, a book written in 1961 by Jane Jacobs. Jacobs strongly believed that the overall strength of American cities largely depends on the interaction between neighbors. Everything that Jacobs wrote in her book was intended to help people feel more connected and more responsible for each other.

PART 4:
HIGHER EVICTIONS AMONG WOMEN THAN MEN AND HOMELESSNESS AMONG CHILDREN

In this part of the book, Desmond writes about how there is a higher rate of eviction among women, especially African-American women. One reason for this is because women are more likely to care for children, and thus have more housing pressure than men.

According to further research, in the 2000s, African-American women accounted for 30 percent of all evicted people, even though African-American women made up only 9 percent of the entire population. One reason for that is because African-American women are even more under-paid than their male counterparts. Other reasons are that men are more able to work all kinds of weird jobs and that in many situations men are more aggressive negotiators. Women often fear negotiating and are ready to settle for less, because the most important thing for many women is to have any job rather than be unemployed.

There is one more thing which makes women more vulnerable than men: women are more likely to have children and when they have children they need bigger homes and more space. A bigger home means higher rent, and in addition, children are noisy and may create all sorts of troubles. There are many situations where landlords evict their tenants for situations like this.

Many children are also homeless. In 2013, approximately one in 30 children in the United States was homeless or had been homeless for at least a year. That is an 8 percent increase from 2012, and between 2006 and 2013 the total number of homeless children increased from 1.5 million to 2.5 million.

Homelessness is particularly prevalent among children of single mothers. But regardless of the cause of homelessness, it has devastating effects on children affected by it. Homeless children are more likely to face the famine and sickness and tend to perform more poorly at school.

After this, Desmond tries to explain why it is so difficult to address child homelessness. He says that it is because many programs intended to help the homeless rarely (if ever) target children directly.

PART 5:
LUCRATIVE RETURN ON PROPERTIES

A landlord who decides to invest money in properties for a relatively low cost and to keep rent high in comparison to the mortgage payment will make a lot of money. Moreover, landlords often do not need to invest a lot of money in maintenance for properties located in poor neighborhoods.

In this way, housing segregation has created many opportunities for landlords who seek chances to become rich by exploiting others. "The Case for Reparations," an essay written in 2014 by Ta-Nehisi Coates, describes examples of such situations. It tells about how in the 1960s, African-American people were denied home financing almost routinely, which led to further segregation and discrimination. They often had no option except to accept deals that were bad for them.

Coates explains how African-American people in 1960s Chicago had to buy houses "on contract." This almost always meant that the buyer gained no equity over it while they were making the payments. If any payment was missed for any reason, the house was lost and the seller could then sell it to his next victim. Sellers thus gained enormous profit because mortgages were denied to African-American people.

Furthermore, Coates agrees that racial discrimination and segregation continues to exist because people benefit from it. Also, a lot of white people know how to use the law to their own benefit and how to cheat both the law and others (in this case, African-Americans) for their own selfish benefit.

The same types of situations occur for many renters today and many of them are African-Americans. And because people are making money off making people poor, it is very difficult to pass laws that would change the conditions which are causing such extreme poverty.

PART 6:
DOMESTIC ABUSE AND FEAR
OF EVICTION

In this chapter, the author discusses the connection between domestic violence and eviction. He states that many women are afraid to file a domestic violence complaint, because when they do, they face eviction because of certain police regulations. For this reason many women fear reporting the violence that is occurring in their own homes, because they does not want end up on the street.

There was an example from Milwaukee between 2008 and 2009 when a woman reported a domestic violence incident to the police. After the police received the report, they issued a nuisance citation to the landlord and demanded that the landlord prevent the nuisance from happening again. Eventually the landlord decided to try to resolve the situation by evicting the tenant. Situations like this are one reason why women fear reporting domestic violence to the authorities. They are afraid of losing their homes and ending up on the street.

Milwaukee is not the only example of a city with nuisance ordinances that serve to punish domestic violence victims. Back in 2013, the American Civil Liberties Union challenged an ordinance in Norristown in Pennsylvania which allowed the municipality to remove a landlord's rental license if three disorderly behavior calls occurred. In short, this meant that if a woman decided to report domestic violence, it would put her landlord at risk of their rental license. And of course, when that risk, the only thing the landlord could do is to evict the tenant.

But Norristown passed a new ordinance, which calls for fines for every disorderly behavior incident. Again, in order to avoid such fines, landlords would simply evict their tenants.

There are many examples where we can see that the poor are often perceived as a nuisance themselves. Because of that, laws are often made to "clear" the poor away and to make them "disappear" rather than to help them and their cause.

PART 7:
THE IMPORTANCE OF HOME

The next chapter is about the importance of the home and the place where we live.

Why is home so important for our lives?

First of all, in our homes we can be honest to who we really are. We can be relaxed, knowing that we are safe and sound in our homes. Homes provide stability, safety and help us realize who we truly are. Homes help us nurture our identity. That is why people who are under constant threat of eviction have no sense of identity or feeling of safety.

Programs intended to help the homeless are mostly aimed at those considered to be the most "deserving." This means that people with addictions may be turned away because they are seen as a threat to the program and to other people. But when it comes to homelessness, instead of trying to "cure the sickness," we should instead focus on "preventing the sickness" in the first place.

One positive example is a program in Utah called Housing First. The main idea is to provide the shelter first and then take care of other problems that people may face, such as addiction. The program from Utah proved very successful. Housing First managed to reduce the number of people who were homeless and who had addictions or mental illness from 2,000 to 200. Also, the Utah model is politically supported thanks to its cost-effectiveness.

PART 8:
ESTABLISHING THE LEGAL AID
FOR THE POOR

Legal aid, especially for the poor, has been in decline for years. Moreover, it was further reduced when the US faced the financial crisis back in 2008. But having legal aid is mandatory, especially for the poor. Without legal aid, the poor cannot get representation. This means that most of them do not have any legal representative in housing courts. In contrast, most landlords (almost 90 percent of them) have legal representatives in court.

According to many studies, if a tenant has a legal representative it is a lot less likely that they will be evicted. In addition, landlords will also be more likely to respect the tenants' rights by reducing charges.

There is an example in New York City, which is slowly moving toward greater legal aid for housing court. It is estimated that New York would spend approximately between 100 and 200 million dollars annually on legal aid for families living below the poverty line. However, New York would also save around 143 million dollars annually on homeless shelter costs if eviction rates were lower, not to mention that the entire city could also save a lot on welfare benefits and the cost of health care.

PART 9:
THE IDEA OF UNIVERSAL HOUSING VOUCHERS

The last part of the book is about housing vouchers. The author claims that current housing vouchers and assistance programs are very limited. Even if a family succeeds in qualifying for such voucher, that does not mean the family will get the aid. According to research, there are more than 20 million people in the United States who have qualified for some form of housing aid but never got any. Back in 2014, there were around 300,000 people on a waitlist in Chicago alone. In 2015, 58,000 people applied for the 105 available affordable homes.

Why is a housing voucher a good idea?

By expanding housing vouchers, many low income people would be included in the help program. This would mean that the eviction rate throughout the entire US would be drastically lowered. This voucher could be used for purchasing housing anywhere, regardless of the neighborhood. Homelessness would be minimal and people would have more money to spend on food and for ensuring better healthcare for them and their families. Also, more people would have the chance to save money.

There are ways to make this happen. One of these ways is cutting housing assistance for the wealthy and getting all the help to those who really need it. According to the Congressional Budget Office, it is estimated that such housing assistance would cost approximately 41 billion dollars over ten years. In the past several years, the United States had spent almost 52 billion dollars in providing housing assistance to those who earn less than 100,000 dollars.

The summary ends here.

ANALYSIS

When we read the book, there are several things immediately visible: the author's neutrality, short, clear sentences, and his aim for a solution. We will explain all of this further below.

Although the book is about stressful situations, such as eviction, poverty, and being poor or even homeless, the author does not dwell too much on that. He does not write about the emotional impact that each of those have on a human being. Instead, the author briefly describes how poverty impacts people and moves on. His clear intention is that bad things are not "everlasting" or simply "how things are," but rather things that can be addressed with practical solutions. But in order to do so, he needs to talk about the problem and to show the entire effect of it. As we read the book, we will see that it is filled with mostly short, straightforward sentences. This is because Desmond did not want to stray from his topic and because he wanted to bring everything to his readers in the simplest way possible. Of course, the entire book is intended to be part of the solution to the poverty and eviction problems that clearly exist, not only in the US, but throughout the world. By providing help for all poor people, not only will the overall situation for the poor eventually change for the better, but also the economic situation of the country as a whole will improve.

QUIZ

Welcome to our short quiz! This quiz is written as a short test for everyone who wants to know more or to repeat everything that they already know about the book. Questions are not difficult and every answer can be found either in summary or 'quiz answers' section. So, let's continue.

QUESTION 1

According to the author, what is the most effective way to help the poor?

a) Lower rents.

b) Universal housing vouchers.

c) Better laws, which would ensure better judicial protection of the poor.

d) Everything above.

QUESTION 2

"According to the author's research, back in _____ an average white person in _____ lived in a neighborhood, which was meant to be more or less- white, with roughly _____ percent of white people living there. In 2016 that number dropped to _____ percent."

QUESTION 3

"According to many studies, if a tenant has legal representative it is a lot less likely that he will be evicted. Not only that, but the landlords will also respect tenant's rights by reducing the charges."

TRUE   FALSE

QUESTION 4

Why is having a legal aid for the poor one of the mandatory things if we want to solve the homelessness issue?

a) If a tenant has a legal aid there is a bigger possibility that his landlord will respect his rights.

b) A tenant with a legal representative has more chances in housing courts that those who does not have any.

c) 'a' and 'b'.

d) Legal aid and better laws will contribute to overall more 'fair' behavior of the landlords because they will fear of paying enormous fees in case of every unlawfulness.

QUESTION 5

"That segregation means many things: one of such examples is connected with_____ being relegated to the North Side and 'white' families being concentrated to the _____."

QUESTION 6

How eviction reflects on a child, especially if that child has only one parent?

a) A child who went through eviction is more likely to perform poor at school.

b) An evicted child may suffer from social phobia, depression and other illnesses.

c) When a child is evicted together with his parents (or a parent) there is a great chance that that child will have great difficulties when trying to fit into the society or having a family on his own.

d) All of the above.

QUESTION 7

Why do women fear to report domestic violence or abuse?

a) They refuse to do so because they are afraid of their husbands.

b) They rarely report their domestic violence because they fear of being thrown out on the street by their landlords.

c) Many women who refuse to report domestic violence do that because they cannot afford legal aid and without it they will lose the dispute.

d) Everything above.

QUIZ ANSWERS

QUESTION 1 – b

QUESTION 2 – "2000, Chicago, 79, 71.5"

QUESTION 3 – TRUE

QUESTION 4 – c

QUESTION 5 – "African-American families, South Side"

QUESTION 6 – d

QUESTION 7 – b

CONCLUSION

Evicted: *Poverty and Profit in the American City* is a book written by American author Matthew Desmond. This book allows us to become better informed about the overall situation regarding evictions and poverty in the American society. As we read the book, we also have the opportunity to read how the judicial system in the US functions when it comes to those who are poor and how many things are aimed toward getting more money for those who already have plenty, leaving nothing for those who are in real, dire need. The book is divided into several chapters, with each chapter explaining one segment of the entire picture. This means that as we read the book, we will slowly learn about the need for a change for the better.

Evicted is written in a simple, conversational style, with many short and straightforward sentences, aiming to bring "the most important" facts to the readers. Because of this, the book is extremely easy and quick to read. But do not think that the book is dull or plain; Desmond managed to write everything he wanted in a way so that all of his readers can easily get the picture and know what he is talking about.

Poverty, homelessness and eviction are our reality and the author presents a lot of practical advice on how to make certain things change for the better. By approaching the issue from a neutral point of view, Desmond succeeded in bringing out what he believes are the most important things we should know.

I believe that *Evicted: Poverty and Profit in the American City* will be a great eye-opener for many people. I also believe that because of that, many people will love the book, just as I did. I recommend reading the book; it is an awakening read that is here to "nudge" us from the comfort of our homes. There are people, even in our own neighborhoods, who need our help and who we can help.

Thank You, and more...

Thank you for spending your time to read this book, I hope now you hold a greater knowledge about '**Evicted.**

Before you go, would you mind leaving us a review on where you purchased your book?

It will mean a lot to us and help us continue making more summaries for you and for others.

Thank you once again!

Yours warmly,

FURTHER READINGS

Here are some other great book's summary

(Just click on it)

1- Summary of Educated: A Memoir by Tara Westover

https://www.amazon.com/dp/B07NXWHK7Q/

2- Summary of Building a StoryBrand by Donald Miller

https://www.amazon.com/dp/B07P1XPTZF/

3- Summary of The Culture Code by Daniel Coyle

https://www.amazon.com/dp/B07P9PRGQT/

4- Summary of Where the Crawdads Sing

https://www.amazon.com/dp/179896998X/

Evicted
A Complete Summary!

Evicted: Poverty and Profit in the American City is
a book written by Matthew Desmond. The book is
about eviction and the side-effects that eviction
can have on a person or community.
Eviction, which involves poverty and the loss of
everything that a person once knew, has an
enormous emotional impact on a person. When
someone loses their home it is hard, if not
impossible, to continue on living, because there are
many things which inevitably follow and none of
them are positive. That is why the author decided
to write about these things that unfortunately
become part of people's lives.

Here is a Preview of What You Will Get:

- A Full Book Summary
- An Analysis
- Fun quizzes
- Quiz Answers
- Etc

Get a copy of this summary and learn about the
ebook.

ISBN 9781090799050

9 781090 799050